The ABCs of Battle

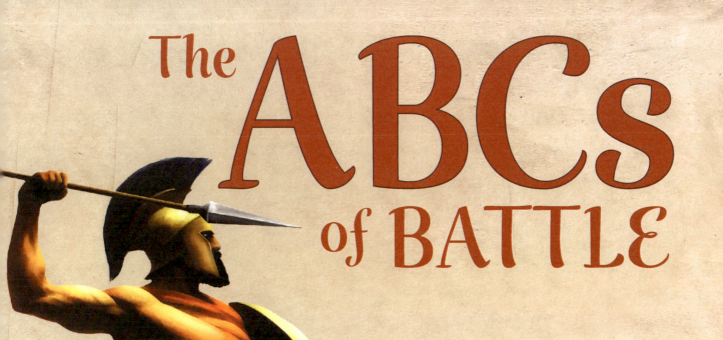

Written by:
Sean Michael Malone

Illustrated by:
Teresa Carlson

Published by Orange Hat Publishing 2024
ISBN PB: 9781645385134
ISBN HC: 9781645385141

Copyrighted © 2024 by Sean Michael Malone
All Rights Reserved
The ABCs of Battles
Written by Sean Michael Malone
Illustrated by Teresa Carlson

This publication and all contents within may not be reproduced or transmitted in any part or in its entirety without the written permission of the author.

www.orangehatpublishing.com

For Erik, Karl, Jakob and Bjorn

And all the Knudson Clan

May the bounds of your imagination

continue to triumph on every battlefield

of your dreams.

A is for Adrianople
August 9, 378

The Romans arrived thirsty and tired.

Unworried, they thought Goths an easy enemy.

Fritigern opposed them, and with horsemen conspired.

Riding through the forest, they surprised Valens' company.

The emperor was slain; the 'barbarians' won the field.

The legions fled, leaving sword, spear, and shield.

 B is for Borodino
September 7, 1812

Napoleon marched with innumerable forces,

Opposed by Cossacks and the great Russian winter.

The French brought guns, wagons, cannons, and horses,

But went home cold, hungry, and bitter.

Bonaparte won that hard-fought battle.

Yet nothing was gained but empty saddles.

C is for Crecy

August 26, 1346

Long ago in the kingdom of France

The English invaded, led by their king.

The French knights charged with sword and lance.

The enemy archers let their longbows sing.

It all seemed over; the French shed tears.

But the war would take one hundred years!

D is for Dunkirk
May 26, 1940

The Second World War was a frightening ordeal.

Cut-off, surrounded, the Allies retreated.

With water before them, Germans on their heels,

It seemed their whole army would soon be defeated!

But then came rescuers in ships, dinghies, and boats

Who picked up the soldiers and kept hope afloat.

# is for Edington
May 9, 878

The King of Wessex was Alfred the Great.

His kingdom was all that remained.

He rallied the Saxons—not a moment too late—

Against a great horde of Vikings and Danes.

Through their stout shield wall, that mighty band

Convinced the island dwellers to call it 'England.'

F is for Falkirk
July 22, 1298

Before their crowns were united

The English and Scots loved to fight.

For independence, the Scots were excited,

And William Wallace had proven his might.

No victory—Falkirk was only painful departure.

The Scots would need new plans to deal with English archers.

G is for Gettysburg
July 1 – 3, 1863

Gettysburg is a place with many hills:

Cemetery, Culp's, Big and Little Round Tops.

Here 'Billy Yank' and 'Johnny Reb' fought to a standstill.

On the third day, Pickett's charge was stopped.

The North held their ground, and the South retreated.

The slaves would be freed, the Confederacy defeated.

is for Hastings
October 14, 1066

King Edward of England died with no heir.

Harold and William each had a claim.

Harold, busy with Vikings, was caught unaware,

Across the 'Channel' from Normandy, William came.

Harold perished, and the rest is history.

The conquest is told in the Bayeux tapestry.

I is for Iwo Jima
February 19 – March 26, 1945

Due south of Japan is a volcanic rock

Only eight square miles, a 'drop' in the sea.

Yet the fiercest fighting took place to unlock

American raiding and air supremacy.

The Japanese were stranded; there could be no retreat.

They stoutly resisted but faced only defeat.

J is for Jutland
May 31 – June 1, 1916

The British blockaded the cold North Sea.

The Germans sent out their fastest vessels.

They baited some battleships and made them debris.

But the British fleet was too big to wrestle.

The Germans were forced back to their port.

Out of options, submarines were their only resort.

is for Kursk
July 5 – August 23, 1943

For two years the Germans and Russians had fought.

The Germans attacked with their new Panther tank.

But the Russians kept their defenses taut.

And they had British spies to thank.

The German plan was uncovered, their defeat no mystery.

The Russians won the largest tank battle in history.

L is for Lexington
(& Concord) April 19, 1775

Boston was a hotbed of revolution.

The British went to seize arms and munitions.

The militia rushed in and saw the solution.

They drove the redcoats from their positions.

The gun smoke had cleared, but still tensions swirled.

That humble skirmish became the "shot heard 'round the world."

M is for Marathon
September 10, 490 BC

The Persians had conquered far and wide.

Their elite 'immortals' were peerless.

Yet Greece remained defiant with pride.

Was it madness, or were they fearless?

The Greeks picked a battlefield that limited enemy movement.

They would repeat this tactic with great improvement.

 is for Nineveh
612 BC

Long ago in Northern Iraq,
Two empires fought for control;
Wielding swords, spears, and slings with rocks,
Claiming Nineveh was their goal.

Assyria and Babylon fought for twelve hard years.
But Babylon won with more allies and peers.

O is for Orleans
October 12, 1428 – May 8, 1429

The English had surrounded the city.

They tried to starve the city with a siege.

But Joan of Arc knew she was more than pretty.

God was on her side; she convinced France and her liege.

A peasant girl inspired the disheartened knights.

The siege was ended, the English out of sight.

P is for Phillipi.
October 3 and 23, 42 BC

Julius Caesar had been killed.

In Rome, a civil war started.

Hail a new Caesar or the Republic rebuild?

The future of many soon would be charted.

The legions fought twice; the liberators were defeated.

Yet between Octavian and Antony, the same drama repeated.

Q is for Quebec
September 13, 1759

For three months the British surrounded Quebec.

At last, the French marched out in a column.

The redcoats were patient, keeping their muskets in check.

They fired their volley, yet became solemn.

Though they had won, General Wolfe gripped his side.

So did French General Montcalm, and neither survived.

# is for Roncevaux Pass
August 15, 778

The Knights of Charlemagne fought a small battle

In the mountains between France and Spain.

The Basques ambushed them on paths made for cattle.

The brave paladin Roland was slain.

Roland's last stand became heroic romance.

A legend was born as the epic of France.

S is for Sekigahara
October 21, 1600

Japan was engulfed in a great civil war.

For more than a century, the samurai battled.

Nobunaga was dead, who had formed the core

Of all sense of unity; the islands were rattled.

At the massive battlefield of Sekigahara,

A new leader triumphed: the Shogun Tokugawa.

T is for Trafalgar
October 21, 1805

In the Cape of Trafalgar, two fleets met.

The Spanish and French had thirty-three ships.

The British had fewer but were all set,

For their Admiral Nelson was well-equipped.

They sailed in two columns and cleaved through the formation.

They lost no ships, but Nelson's death shocked the nation.

is for Ulundi
July 4, 1879

The British colonies in Africa were large.

They clashed with many peoples and tribes.

The Zulus shocked them with the force of their charge,

So the redcoat army was tripled in size.

Their guns and cannons dominated the terrain

And the Zulu Kingdom became another British domain.

V is for Vienna
September 12, 1683

The Ottoman Empire was near the height of its power

And attacked Vienna with a multitude of troops.

They attacked the Holy League at the fourth hour

To prevent the relief cavalry from forming in groups.

But with a great charge came the Polish at the center.

The city was saved; the Ottomans did not enter.

is for Waterloo
June 18, 1815

Napoleon was desperate; his time was pressed.

First beat the British, then the Prussians was the plan.

So he fired the cannons and sent his best of the best.

But the redcoats were tough; not one man ran.

The Duke of Wellington their praises did sing.

The battle was close; he called it "a near-run thing."

X is for Xiaoting
Autumn, 221

China was divided; three kingdoms laid claim.

Each sought control: Wu, Shu, and Wei.

On the Yangtze's shores, Wu and Shu armies came.

For months there was stalemate, until a fateful day.

The Wu lit straw piles on fire to burn the Shu tents.

With their camp destroyed, the Shu went!

Y is for Yarmuk

August 15 – 20, 636

Yarmuk is a river in Jordan's desert.

There, Arabs battled the eastern Romans.

Each were inspired by faith and great effort.

But fighting started slow, full of retreats and ill omens.

But after six days, the determined Arabs won.

They had proven their new age would not be undone.

Z is for Zama
October 19, 202 BC

Hannibal of Carthage had crossed into Italy.

His elephants left many legions deceased.

But after, the war had not gone prettily.

Scipio of Rome blew horns to frighten the beasts.

Scipio beat Hannibal; the Numidians proved vital.

The Senate declared Africanus as his new title.

War is a terrible thing, full of harsh realities. Throughout history, soldiers who have fought in wars have often repeated that there is nothing glorious about it. At the same time, the motivations that inspired soldiers to go to battle, the accounts of the conflict, and tales of heroism and sacrifice have never failed to captivate historians and the general public alike. The history of warfare speaks to all cultures and audiences, and being ignorant of such battles is a worse disservice than to risk romanticizing them. This book has been presented as a fun, educational resource—for the young learner, history buff, and trivia nerd alike.

SEAN MICHAEL MALONE is an author living in Waukesha Wisconsin, with his wife Athena and his three daughters- Evangeline, Frances, and Mathilde, and Shetland Sheepdog Simonsen. He has previously published Lovecraftian novels *Spring City Terror* and *Ocean's Grave*. *The ABCs of Battle* is his first book for early readers, and taps into his love for military history that began with Age of Empires II on the PC. He continues to write fiction inspired by history and myth. For more from Sean, visit his author website at seanmaloneauthor.com.

TERESA CARLSON hails from the picturesque landscapes of Wisconsin and has been an illustrator and designer for over two decades. Her journey began with hand-drawn sketches and paintings. As technology evolved, so did her artistry. Teresa strives to seamlessly blend the tactile feel of traditional media with the boundless possibilities of digital tools, whether it's whimsical characters, beautiful landscapes, or thought-provoking visual narratives. In this wonderful book, every stroke is an invitation for the reader to step into a world where history takes shape and ideas are brought to life.

Milton Keynes UK
Ingram Content Group UK Ltd.
UKRC032235071024
449408UK00013B/112